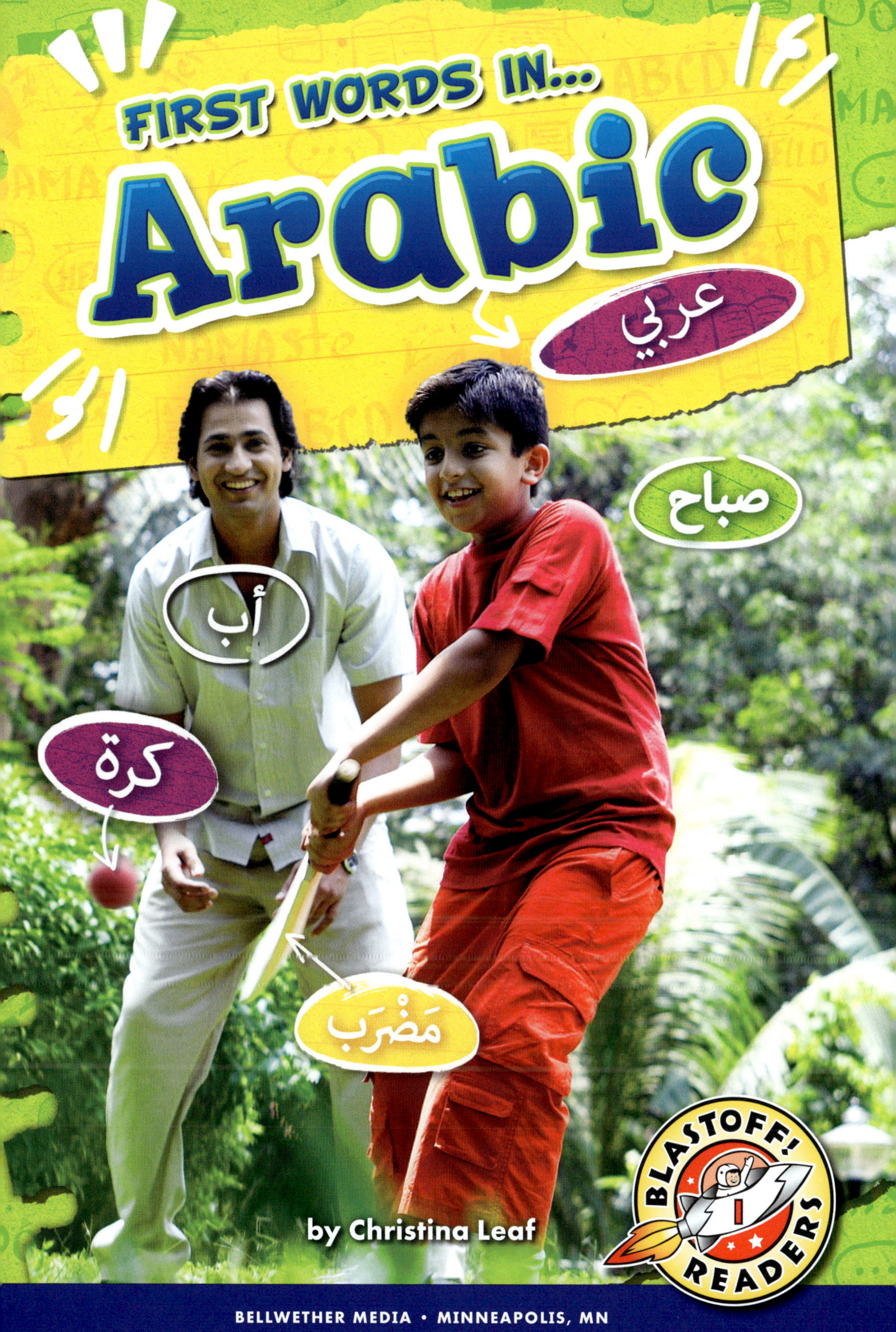
FIRST WORDS IN...
Arabic
عربي
صباح
أب
كرة
مَضْرَب
by Christina Leaf
BLASTOFF! READERS
1
BELLWETHER MEDIA • MINNEAPOLIS, MN

Blastoff! Readers are carefully developed by literacy experts to build reading stamina and move students toward fluency by combining standards-based content with developmentally appropriate text.

Level 1 provides the most support through repetition of high-frequency words, light text, predictable sentence patterns, and strong visual support.

Level 2 offers early readers a bit more challenge through varied sentences, increased text load, and text-supportive special features.

Level 3 advances early-fluent readers toward fluency through increased text load, less reliance on photos, advancing concepts, longer sentences, and more complex special features.

★ **Blastoff! Universe**

Reading Level

Grade K

Grades 1–3

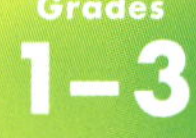

Grade 4

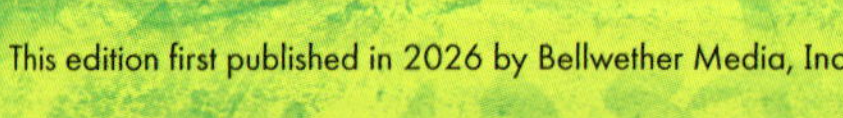

This edition first published in 2026 by Bellwether Media, Inc.

Library of Congress Cataloging-in-Publication Data

LC record for Arabic available at: https://lccn.loc.gov/2025019030

Editor: Suzane Nguyen Designer: Andrea Schneider

Printed in the United States of America, North Mankato, MN.

Table of Contents

Marhaban!

Marhaban!
I am Khaled.
I speak Arabic.
Let's learn to
speak together!

Words to Know

- اسمي... ismee (ISS-me)..........my name is
- نَعَم..... nem (NAHam)...........................yes
- لا .... laa (leh) ....no
- مِن فَضلِكَ...min fadlak (MIN fahd-lik-ah) ....please (to a male)
- مِن فَضلِكِ...min fadlik (MIN fahd-lik-ee).. ....please (to a female)

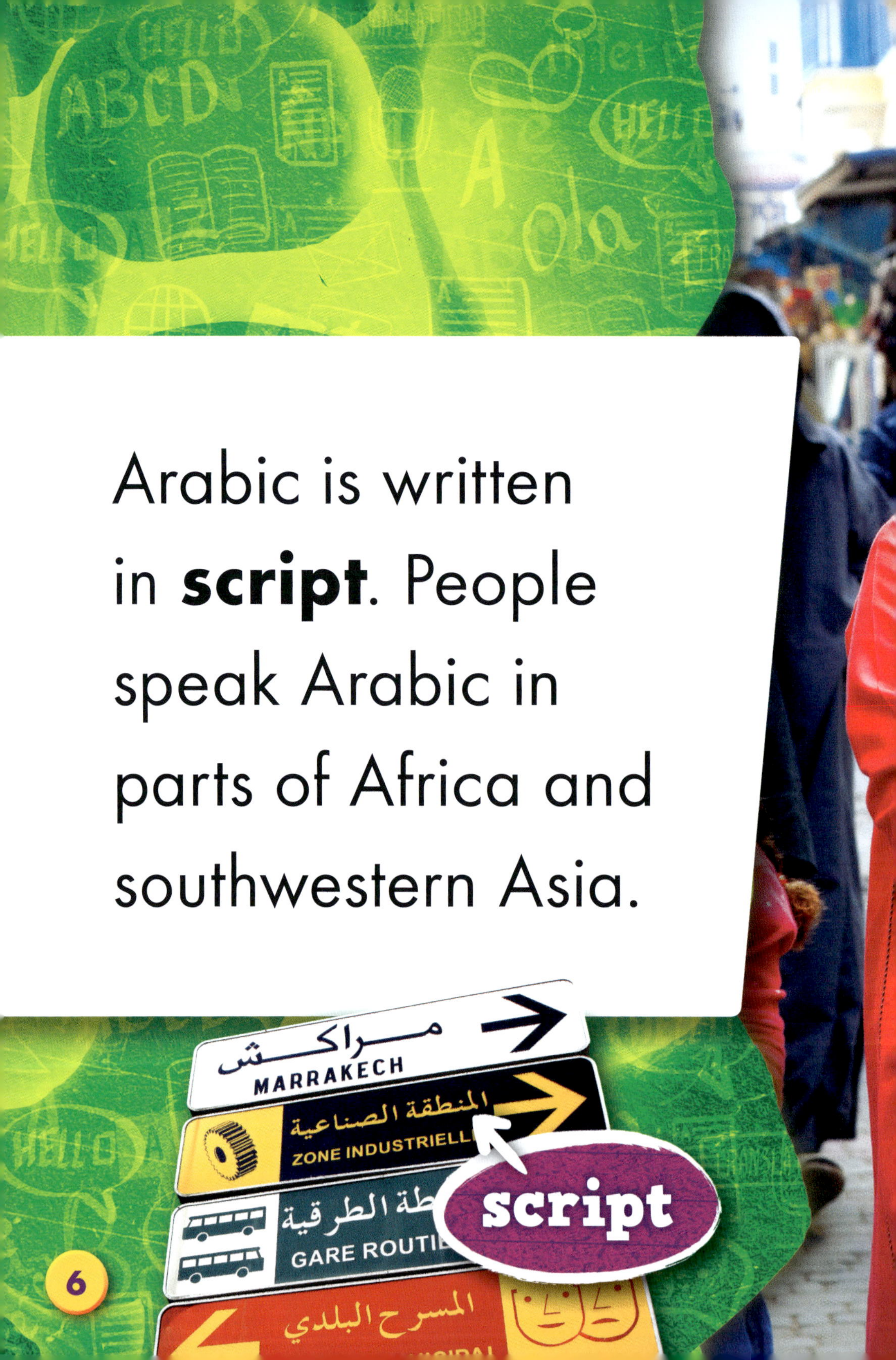

Arabic is written in **script**. People speak Arabic in parts of Africa and southwestern Asia.

Arabic-speaking Countries
Asia
Africa

Aryan's *`aa `ilah* is **Muslim**. They pray each *sabaah*. He has his own **prayer rug**.

Words to Know
• عائلة ..... 'aa 'ilah (ah IL-ah) .... family
• أُمّ .... 'um (oohm) .... mother
• أبّ .... 'ab (ahb)............................... father
• مسلم ....(MOOS-leem) .... Muslim
• صباح.....sabaah (sah-BAH) .... morning
'ab

Zara's mother makes **balaleet** for *futoor*. They eat sweet dates, too.

Words to Know

- فُطور ....futoor (fuh-TOOR)......... **breakfast**
- أخّ ....'akh (ahkh) .... **brother**
- أُخْت ....'ukht (uhkt) .... **sister**
- مطبخ ...matbakh (MAHT-bahk) .....**kitchen**
- كرسي ....kursee (KUR-see).................**chair**
- طاولة ...taawila (TAH-WEE-leh)........ **table**

At School

Aria practices writing at *madrasa*. Her *mudaris* helps her. They write script right to left!

waraq

Count in Arabic

١.... waahid (WAH-hed).... 1
٢... ithnaan (ITH-nayn)....... 2
٣... talaata (tah-LAY-tah).. 3
٤... arba'ah (ar-BAH-ah)....... 4
٥... khamsa (KHAM-sah).. 5
٦... sitta (SIT-tah)............... 6
٧... sabaa (sah-BAH)........ 7
٨... tamanya (tah-MAN-eya).. 8
٩... tisaa (teh-SAH)...... 9
١٠.. ashrah (AH-sha-rah).... 10

mudaris

Words to Know

- مدرسة... madrasa (mah-DRE-sah) .... school
- مدرس.... mudaris (moo-dah-REES) .... teacher
- مَكْتَب.... maktab (MAK-tahb)............. desk
- وَرَق...... waraq (wah-RAHK) .... paper

Time for *ghada*! Fatima eats with her *sadiquati*.

Words to Know
• صَديق..... sadiq (sah-DEEK).. friend (male)
• صديقة ... sadiqa (sah-DEE-kah) .... friend (female)
• صديقتي .. sadiquati (sah-DEEK-kwah-ti) .. .. friends
• غَذاء....... ghada (gha-DAY)................. lunch
• طَعام...... ta'aam (tah-AHM)................. food
• كوب ...... kub (KOOB)............................ cup
sadiqa
kub

After School

Saeed plays *karikit* after school. His *alfariq* wins the *mubara*!

Words to Know

- كريكيت .. **karikit** (kah-REE-kee-et) .. **cricket**
- الفريق .... **alfariq** (ahl-fahr-EEK) .... **team**
- مُباراة ..... **mubara** (moo-BAHR-ah) ...... **match**
- كُرة .... **koora** (COO-rah) .... **ball**
- مَضْرَب .... **madrab** (MAH-drahb) .... **bat**

Amira eats lamb and *urz* for *asha*.

Words to Know

- أُرْز ....urz (OOR-zuh) .... **rice**
- عشاء .....asha (ah-SHA) .... **dinner**
- ملْعَقة....mil'aqah (MILL-lahk-ah)..... **spoon**
- شَوْكة.....shooka (SHOH-kah) .... **fork**
- سِكّين.....sik-keen (sih-KIN)................ **knife**

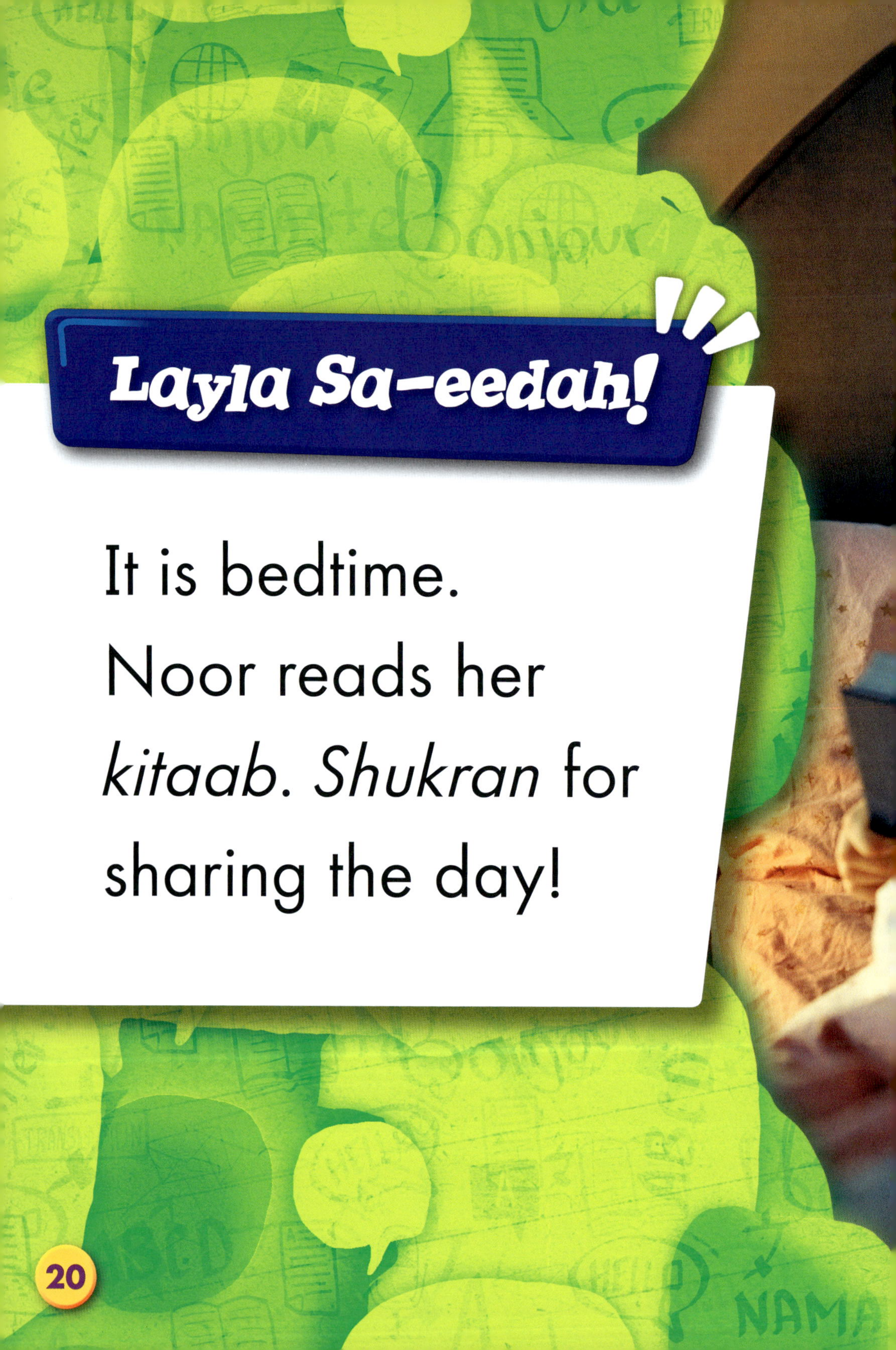

Layla Sa-eedah!

It is bedtime. Noor reads her *kitaab*. *Shukran* for sharing the day!

Words to Know

- شُكرًا ....shukran (SHOO-kran)..thank you
- كِتاب ....kitaab (KEY-tahb) .... book
- مَعَ السَّلامة .....maa as-salaama ....(mah-a sah-LAH-mah)...............goodbye

Glossary

balaleet

a dish made with noodles and eggs

prayer rug

a rug used by Muslims to kneel and pray on

Muslim

people of the Islamic faith

script

the way of writing Arabic

To Learn More

AT THE LIBRARY

Davies, Monika. *Egypt*. Minneapolis, Minn.: Bellwether Media, 2023.

Farag, Islam Medhat. *Arabic Picture Dictionary*. Tokyo, Japan: Tuttle Publishing, 2024.

Ruurs, Margriet. *Stepping Stones: A Refugee Family's Journey*. Victoria, B.C.: Orca Book Publishers, 2016.

ON THE WEB

FACTSURFER

Factsurfer.com gives you a safe, fun way to find more information.

1. Go to www.factsurfer.com.
2. Enter "Arabic" into the search box and click 🔍.
3. Select your book cover to see a list of related content.

Index

The images in this book are reproduced through the courtesy of: Fuse/ Getty Images, front cover; Pixel-Shot, p. 3; FG Trade, pp. 4-5; Hisham Ibrahim/ Getty Images, p. 6 (script); Zzvet, pp. 6-7; Aisha, p. 8 (prayer rug); nazar_ab/ Getty Images, pp. 8-9; Fayisbi, p. 10 (balaleet); ibnjaafar, pp. 10-11; Miltan, p. 12 (waraq); kenchiro168, pp. 12-13; Thanh, p. 14 (ta'aam); SolStock/ Getty Images, pp. 14-15; WESTOCK PRODUCTIONS, pp. 16-17; MaraZe, p. 18 (shooka); Drazen, pp. 18-19; Konstantin Yuganov, pp. 20-21; Pretti, p. 22 (balaleet); LightField Studios, p. 22 (Muslim); Cultura Creative, p. 22 (prayer rug); New Africa, p. 22 (script).